Rats Incredible

An Illustrated Dictionary of Rats

Ryn Gargulinski

WEISERBOOKS

Boston, MA/York Beach, ME

Boston, MA/York Beach, ME
First published in 2006 by
Red Wheel/Weiser, LLC
York Beach, ME
With offices at:
368 Congress Street
Boston, MA 02210
www.redwheelweiser.com

Library of Congress Cataloging-in-Publication Data

Gargulinski, Ryn.
  Rats incredible! : an illustrated dictionary of rats / Ryn Gargulinski.
      p. cm.
  ISBN 1-57863-370-2
  1. Rats—Humor. I. Title.
PN6231.R354G37 2006
818'.602—dc22

                                        2005030523

Typeset in Berliner Grotesk and Ashley Script by Elizabeth Wood

Printed in China
C&C

13 12 11 10 09 08 07 06
  8 7 6 5 4 3 2 1

inaugu-rat-ion

Myth: Rats eat small children.
Reality: Rats eat only dead small children, prefer dog food to cheese, and prefer spaghetti sauce over just about anything.

Myth: Rats have rabies.
Reality: Junkies have rabies.

Myth: Rats are filthy.
Reality: Rats are some of the cleanest creatures on earth. They bathe themselves, like cats, and even wash behind their ears. Unlike cats, they are also not as averse to water (although one rat did cry like a banshee when subjected to a shiny coat shampoo).

Myth: Rats are mean and want to hurt you.

Reality: Rats are just like any other of God's creatures—more scared of humans than we are of them. This is not to say you should go stick your hand in a sewer and make a clicking noise, but don't close your mind to owning a domestic one. Rats make some of the finest pets: they are intelligent, loving, and can even be taught to play basketball.

Myth: "You look like rat puke" is an insult.

Reality: Rats cannot puke (the reason they are so susceptible to poison).

See?

Rats really **are** incredible!

① Thin, swift tail with the ability to shed its sheath if caught in a doorway.

② Perky little ears, all the better with which to hear cheese wrappers.

③ Wispy whiskers that quiver when they sense danger.

④ Tempting teeth that grow forever lest they chew on a tough substance (like a diamond).

⑤ Beady little eyes best used in the dark.

⑥ Pretty paws with three fingers and a thumb-like appendage; used to hold walnuts, climb fences and open doors.

⑦ Beatific and bounteous body, both supple and firm; can stretch through a teeny hole that fits just their head.

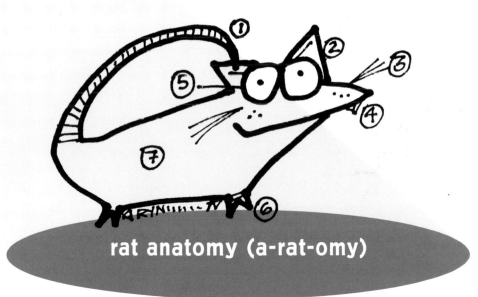

rat anatomy (a-rat-omy)

alas... i knew him well...

"By gnawing through a dike,
even a rat may drown a nation."

–Edmund Burke (1729-1797)

ado-rat-ion
extreme affection, like rats have
for spaghetti sauce.

b-rat
a sassy, incorrigible beast that likes
to bite and pee on carpets—
most rats are not brats; most hamsters are.

b-rat-wurst
a German sausage stuffed with German stuff
and favored by non-German rats who
didn't grow up with it.

ca-rat
a measurement of that saucy diamond with
which all good rats should be rewarded; or, that
orange thing not just for rabbits anymore.

celeb-rat-e

something you do with cake when your rat
has a birthday, graduation, or just learned
how to tie a shoe.

corpo-rat-e
a mindless rat in a suit who joined the rat race.

deco-rat-e
what you do with bulbs on trees or with purple
cushions and miniature Dalí reproductions
in every rat cage.

d-rat
polite form of "damn" or the F-word; a mild
curse used by rats from loving homes.

e-rat-icate (sic)
what rats want to do to those annoying subway
trains that infringe upon their tracks and tunnels.

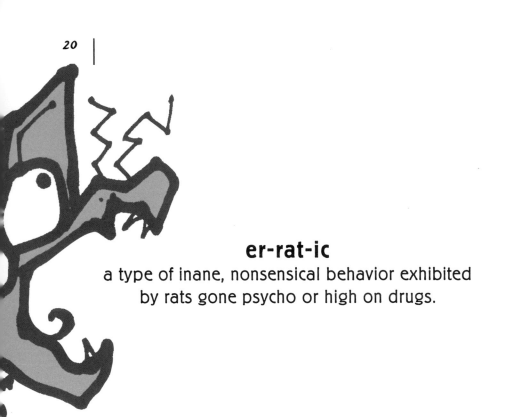

er-rat-ic
a type of inane, nonsensical behavior exhibited
by rats gone psycho or high on drugs.

f-rat-ernity
a wild, unruly gang of rats who wear matching
T-shirts and guzzle beer.

g-rat-itude
the overwhelming joy you feel when
your pet rat licks you.

Ho-rat-io
Shakespearean character played by a skull;
since rats like to dig they meet him often.

i-rat-e
extreme anger shown when your rat bangs his
empty water bottle you neglected to fill.

ir-rat-ional
when rats do weird and senseless things—
like bolt into a cat den or follow the Pied Piper.

Ma-rat
a rat made famous by being murdered
in his bathtub and immortalized by
painter Jacques-Louis David.

mole rat
species of rat that most resembles
Mae West or Marilyn Monroe.

o-rat-e
a way to clear out a large room of people
by simply opening your mouth; rats don't need
to do this to do the clearing.

pi-rat-e

vagabond rats with one leg, a hook hand, and a
squawky pet bird; they like to pillage mice ships.

p-rat-tle
what housewives do on the phone or city rats
do when they run across a long lost
country rat cousin.

ak-Yak yak yak yak-Yak yak yak yak-Yak yak yak Yak

rat hole

a hole in a rat; a rat in a hole; where rats putt their ball on a golf course.

rat pack
a pack of rats; a pack worn by rats;
a rat's favorite brand of cigarettes.

rats' bane
a form of arsenic used against rats, especially
by old women in antique lace.

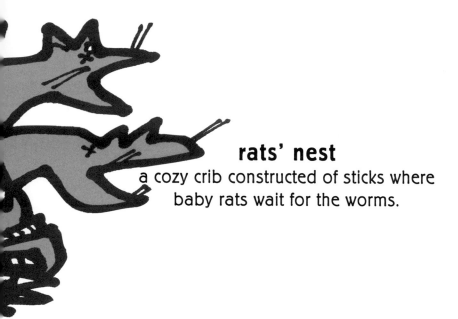

rats' nest
a cozy crib constructed of sticks where
baby rats wait for the worms.

rat-afia
a cordial made of fruit rinds found by rats
in a restaurant dumpster.

rat-a-tat
the sound of a rat on a drum; the sound of a rat
with that empty water bottle you neglected to fill.

rat-atouille
a thick stew made of vegetable rinds found
by rats in a restaurant dumpster.

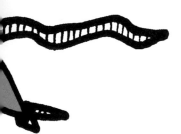

rat-her
what a rat would be doing if he
weren't stuck in a cage.

rat-ion
a rat's daily allocation of food.

rat-tan
wicker-like substance great for
sitting or chewing on.

rat-tle
what baby rats shake when they are too
young to bang the water bottle.

sc-rat-ch

what rats do to walls or Formica if they skid.

st-rat-osphere
where all good rats go when they die.

t-rat-toria
a small, inexpensive Italian restaurant that
specializes in rats' favorite dishes:
anything with spaghetti sauce.

w-rat-h
what rabid rats and bitten humans have.

about the author/artist

Ryn Gargulinski is a writer, poet, artist, and humorist who is currently blessed with one pet rodent, a solid black rambunctious rat named Little Man. Ryn once reigned over an entire award-winning rodent empire. One of her finest, Doctor Eric Joshua III, Esq., was mentioned in the *Wall Street Journal* after gnashing his way to "Best Pet" honors. In her rat-breeding days, Ryn also served as the President of the Northeast Rat & Mouse Club's New York Chapter. Ryn chewed her way through studies resulting in a BFA in Creative Writing, an MA in English Literature, and a thesis on subway folklore. She spends her time creating and yearning to live in France. You can find samples of her columns, poems, illustrations, and photos—all of which have appeared in numerous publications—on her website at *ryngargulinski.com*. She is also author/illustrator of four chapbooks, several illustrated humor books, a series of children's books, and President of RYN-dustries. You can buy her art at *cafeshops.com/ryndustries*. Also, you can smile at a rat and make her happy. Contact her at *ryngargulinski@hotmail.com*.